Classy Casseroles

A Recipe Collection
Jackie Gannaway

Published in Austin, TX by COOKBOOK CUPBOARD
P.O. Box 50053, Austin, TX 78763
(512) 477-7070 phone   (512) 891-0094 fax

ISBN 1-885597-23-1

Artwork by Mosey 'N Me   1436 Baird, Katy, TX 77493

Mail Order Information

To order a copy of this book send a check for $3.95 + $1.50 for shipping (TX residents add 8 % sales tax) to Cookbook Cupboard, P.O. Box 50053, Austin, TX 78763. Send a note asking for this title by name. If you would like a descriptive list of all the fun titles in The Kitchen Crafts Collection, send a note asking for an order blank. Other books you might enjoy are "A Month of Menus", 30 dinners with step by step instructions and even grocery lists!, "Cake Mix Cakes", 40 cakes that start with a purchased cake mix, "The Thanksgiving Table", everything you need to cook Thanksgiving dinner - many recipes. All the Kitchen Crafts titles are $3.95. There is only one shipping charge of $1.50 per order.

Table of Contents

Introduction

Casseroles - dinner in a dish! Great to take to potlucks, welcome a new neighbor, help a sick friend, feed your family for a week and dress up for company.

This book has many of America's favorite casseroles, lowered in fat, streamlined with convenience foods and even a *secret* for keeping the casserole dish clean!

Three brunch casseroles and three dessert casseroles are included for good measure (and good eating). (The desserts can even cook in the oven along with dinner.)

Give this book as a shower gift with one of the nice thermal casserole carriers and some oven mitts!

The following information is given for each recipe:

Make ahead? Tells if any or all of the casserole can be prepared the day before - good for party planning.

Freeze leftovers? Freeze and label individual portions in quart freezer bags. They will be at their best for 1 month. To serve, pierce bag and microwave for 3 minutes or so.

Serve with: Casseroles are very filling so only light additional food is called for. I usually suggest a salad (I love the "salad in a bag" available now in the produce sections. Some are just assorted lettuces, while some are kits with croutons and salad dressing included.)

A green vegetable is good. gelain salads are good because they are cold and sweet, a good contrast to the casserole. They are also easy to carry along with the casserole to a potluck. Fruit and fruit salads are also good choices. Serving simple fruit, salad or plain green vegetables helps lower the fat content of the whole meal.

Optional Garnish: Garnishes are added for the last 5 - 10 minutes of cooking time and nicely dress up a dish for company. (Except for parsley which is added after the dish is cooked.)

Casserole Dish

Most of these recipes call for a 9" x 13" pan. If you use a different dish, you will need one that holds 3 quarts (12 cups). If it is a deep dish you will probably cook the casserole a little longer at a lower temperature.

Convenience Foods

Purchased grated cheese. The bags are marked in ounces:

16 oz. = 1 lb. = 4 cups grated cheese.

12 oz. = 3/4 lb. = 3 cups grated cheese.

8 oz. = 1/2 lb. = 2 cups grated cheese.

Velveeta® cheese is available grated, also.

Boneless, Skinless Chicken Breasts

This convenience food serves two purposes. It is lower in fat and easier to boil and chop than a whole chicken.

A little less than 1/2 lb. of boneless, skinless chicken breast = 1 cup cooked chopped meat.

3 boneless, skinless chicken breasts is about right for a casserole. It is about 1 1/4 lbs. which yields about 3 cups. Casseroles are forgiving in the exact quantities of meat used. A little more or less won't significantly change the casserole.

Lower Fat

These recipes were written with low fat ingredients where they could be used. The meat and cheese are high in fat. Using some lower fat ingredients where they won't be noticed helps lower the overall fat.

How to Boil Chicken

Place the boneless, skinless chicken breasts into boiling water. Simmer about 20 minutes. Add onions and celery to the water for better flavor. Save the broth and freeze it. Boil and chop several meals worth of chicken at one time. Chop and freeze the extra (3 cups each in freezer bags).

Boil a whole chicken the same way. It will take about 35 to 45 minutes. Cool the cooked chicken and remove the skin, Pull off the meat and chop it. Do 2 or 3 chickens and freeze the meat as described above.

The Secret to Keeping the Casserole Dish Clean

Buy Reynolds® brand (as in Reynolds.Wrap®) "Small Oven Cooking Bags". These are oven proof plastic. Cut open up one side and across the end. Lay this rectangle in the casserole dish with the edges hanging over the sides. It is not necessary to spray or grease the plastic wrap. The casserole dish will be almost as clean when you are through as it was when you started.

Chicken and Dressing

1 1/2 sticks margarine
1 (10 oz.) frozen bag Bird's Eye® "Vegetables for
    Seasoning" (this is a blend of onions, celery and
    bell pepper)
  (OR 1 cup chopped onion and 1 cup chopped celery)
1 to 1 1/2 tsp. sage
1 tsp. pepper
6 cups chicken broth, divided
1 (8 oz.) canister cornbread stuffing mix
4 boneless, skinless chicken breasts, cooked and
    chopped, (4 cups) (1 1/2 lbs.) (be sure to save
    6 cups broth to use in recipe)
4 boiled eggs, sliced

1. Place margarine in very large nonstick pan.
   Melt over medium heat. Add bag of seasoning
   vegetables (or onion and celery).
   Sauté 10 minutes, stirring often.
2. Add 4 cups chicken broth. Bring to a boil.
3. Add dry stuffing mix, sage and pepper.
   Mix well. Cover and immediately turn off heat.
   Let stand 5 minutes.
4. Place half stuffing in a sprayed 9" x 13" baking dish.
5. Cover with chopped cooked chicken and sliced eggs.
6. Top with remaining stuffing.
7. Pour 2 cups of chicken broth evenly over all.
8. Bake uncovered 30 minutes at 350° (325°- glass
   pan).

8 - 10 servings.

Make ahead? No.

Freeze leftovers? Yes.

Serve with: Cranberry sauce, English peas with
mushrooms and pearl onions, dinner rolls.

Optional Garnish: Fresh parsley.

6

Chicken Spaghetti

2 quarts water
4 boneless skinless chicken breasts, (1 1/2 lbs.)
1 (16 oz.) pkg. vermicelli
1 stick margarine
1 green bell pepper, chopped
1 medium onion, chopped
1/2 tsp. Worcestershire sauce
16 oz. Light Velveeta®, cubed or grated, (4 cups)
    (or buy grated Velveeta®)
1 (10 oz.) can Rotel® tomatoes and green chilies
1 (4 oz.) can mushroom stems and pieces, drained

1. Bring water to a boil and add chicken breasts.
   Boil gently until chicken is tender. Remove
   chicken from pan, reserving broth. Chop chicken.
2. Bring broth back to a boil and cook vermicelli.
3. While vermicelli is cooking, melt margarine in
   nonstick skillet. Add bell pepper and onion.
   Sauté 5 minutes, stirring constantly.
   Add Worcestershire sauce.
4. Drain vermicelli. Add cheese to hot vermicelli.
   Stir to melt cheese.
5. Add mushrooms, peppers and onions.
6. Place mixture in 9" x 13" baking dish.
7. Bake uncovered 20 to 30 minutes at 300°
   (275° glass pan).

6 - 8 servings.

Make ahead? Can be made a day ahead. Refrigerate.
Let come to room temperature 30 minutes before
heating. If it is not hot after baking 30 minutes,
cover with foil and continue heating.

Freeze leftovers? Yes.

Serve with: A salad kit in a bag (honey mustard
dressing would be good), crescent rolls sprinkled
with grated Parmesan before rolling up and baking.

Optional Garnish: Sliced black olives.

Chicken Cashew Casserole

2 Tb. margarine
1/4 cup chopped onion
1 cup chopped celery
2/3 cup chicken broth
2 (10 oz.) cans low fat cream of mushroom soup
3 boneless, skinless chicken breasts, cooked and
    chopped (3 cups) (save broth)
3 Tb. light soy sauce
2 cups cooked rice (3/4 cup rice before cooking)
1 cup chopped cashews
3/4 cup chow mein noodles

1. Place margarine in large nonstick skillet.
    Sauté onion and celery 5 minutes, stirring often.
2. Add broth and soup. Mix well. Simmer 5 minutes.
3. Add chicken and soy sauce. Simmer 5 minutes.
4. Mix in cooked rice.
5. Place in well sprayed 8" square or 9" square
    baking pan.
6. Bake uncovered 20 minutes at 350° (325°- glass
    pan).
7. Sprinkle cashews and chow mein noodles over
    top. Bake 10 more minutes.

6 - 8 servings.

Make ahead? Can be partly assembled a day ahead. Prepare chicken mixture and cook rice, but don't mix them until just before baking.

Freeze leftovers? No (because of topping).

Serve with: Spinach "salad in a bag", with sliced boiled eggs, Catalina dressing and a few cashews and chow mein noodles tossed in. Also serve with hot soft breadsticks (dairy case).

Optional Garnish: This one is already garnished.

Chicken Broccoli Rice Casserole

1 cup chopped onion
1 cup chopped green bell pepper
1 (10 oz.) can low fat cream of mushroom soup or
 Campbell's® Mushroom Soup with Roasted Garlic
1 (16 oz.) jar Cheez Whiz®
3 cups cooked rice (1 cup uncooked rice before cooking)
1 (16 oz.) bag frozen chopped broccoli, thawed (use a good
 brand of broccoli - and cut stems into smaller pieces)
3 boneless, skinless chicken breasts, cooked and chopped
 (3 cups) (1 1/4 lbs.)

1. Sauté onion and green pepper in large sprayed
 nonstick skillet for 5 minutes, stirring constantly.
2. Stir in soup and cheese. Heat over low heat, stirring
 constantly until creamy.
3. Place rice, broccoli and chicken in large bowl. Mix well.
4. Place half the rice mixture in well sprayed 9" x 13"
 baking dish. Top with half the cheese mixture. Repeat.
5. Bake uncovered 30 minutes at 350° (325°- glass pan).

6 - 8 servings.

Make ahead? No.

Freeze leftovers? Yes.

Serve with: Fresh strawberries, bananas and kiwi
with poppyseed dressing (purchased) or gelatin salad.

Optional Garnish: Sesame seeds or fresh parsley.

9

Golden Cornbread Casserole

1 lb. extra lean ground beef
1 small onion, chopped
1/3 cup picante sauce
1/2 tsp. garlic powder
1/2 tsp. each salt and pepper
2 (6 oz.) packets cornbread mix
eggs
skim milk or low fat buttermilk
6 oz. Cheddar cheese, grated (1 1/2 cups)

1. Brown ground beef and onion in medium non-stick pan. Drain off fat.
2. Add picante and seasonings.
3. Mix cornbread packets in large bowl with the amount of eggs and milk called for on packets.
4. Pour more than half the cornbread batter into well sprayed 9" x 13" baking dish.
5. Place meat mixture evenly over cornbread. Top with 1 cup grated Cheddar.
6. Pour remaining cornbread mixture over meat and top with remaining Cheddar.
7. Bake uncovered at 20 minutes at 400° (375°- glass pan) until cornbread is lightly browned.

6 - 8 servings.

Make ahead? No.

Freeze leftovers? No.

Serve with: Mexican style "salad in a bag" with chopped green onions and Ranch dressing.

Optional Garnish: Grated Parmesan cheese.

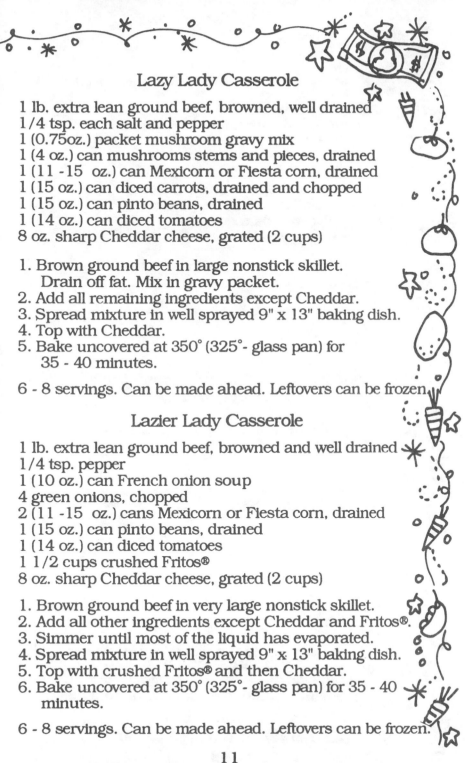

Lazy Lady Casserole

1 lb. extra lean ground beef, browned, well drained
1/4 tsp. each salt and pepper
1 (0.75oz.) packet mushroom gravy mix
1 (4 oz.) can mushrooms stems and pieces, drained
1 (11 -15 oz.) can Mexicorn or Fiesta corn, drained
1 (15 oz.) can diced carrots, drained and chopped
1 (15 oz.) can pinto beans, drained
1 (14 oz.) can diced tomatoes
8 oz. sharp Cheddar cheese, grated (2 cups)

1. Brown ground beef in large nonstick skillet.
   Drain off fat. Mix in gravy packet.
2. Add all remaining ingredients except Cheddar.
3. Spread mixture in well sprayed 9" x 13" baking dish.
4. Top with Cheddar.
5. Bake uncovered at 350° (325°- glass pan) for
   35 - 40 minutes.

6 - 8 servings. Can be made ahead. Leftovers can be frozen.

Lazier Lady Casserole

1 lb. extra lean ground beef, browned and well drained
1/4 tsp. pepper
1 (10 oz.) can French onion soup
4 green onions, chopped
2 (11 -15 oz.) cans Mexicorn or Fiesta corn, drained
1 (15 oz.) can pinto beans, drained
1 (14 oz.) can diced tomatoes
1 1/2 cups crushed Fritos®
8 oz. sharp Cheddar cheese, grated (2 cups)

1. Brown ground beef in very large nonstick skillet.
2. Add all other ingredients except Cheddar and Fritos®.
3. Simmer until most of the liquid has evaporated.
4. Spread mixture in well sprayed 9" x 13" baking dish.
5. Top with crushed Fritos® and then Cheddar.
6. Bake uncovered at 350° (325°- glass pan) for 35 - 40
   minutes.

6 - 8 servings. Can be made ahead. Leftovers can be frozen.

Chicken Enchilada Casserole

3 boneless, skinless chicken breasts, cooked and
    chopped (3 cups) (1 1/4 lbs.)
1 (10 oz.) can low fat cream of celery soup
1 (10 oz.) can low fat cream of chicken soup
1 (12 oz. can) evaporated skim milk
1 (4 oz. can) chopped green chilies
8 corn tortillas, torn into quarters
8 oz. Velveeta® cheese, grated (2 cups)
    (or buy grated Velveeta®)

1. Mix first 6 ingredients in large bowl. Place one third
   of this mixture into sprayed 9" x 13" baking dish.
2. Top with half the tortilla pieces.
3. Repeat with one more third chicken mixture and
   remaining tortillas.
4. Top with remaining chicken. Spread Velveeta® evenly
   over top.
5. Cover with foil. Bake 45 minutes at 350° (325°- glass
   pan). Allow to set in pan 15 minutes before serving.

6 - 8 servings.

Make ahead? No.

Freeze leftovers? Yes.

Serve with: Tomato halves stuffed with guacamole.
Cut a large tomato in half. Slice a small piece off the
bottom so it will sit flat. Scoop out and discard seeds.
Drain upside down on paper towels. Fill with guacamole
(homemade or dairy case or frozen). Hot French bread
loaf - dairy case.

Optional Garnish: Sliced black olives.

12

King Ranch Casserole

1 (10 oz.) can low fat cream of mushroom soup or
    Campbell's® Mushroom Soup with Roasted Garlic
1 (10 oz.) can low fat cream of chicken soup
1/2 cup chicken broth
1 (10 oz.) can Rotel® diced tomatoes and green chilies
3 boneless, skinless chicken breasts, cooked and
    chopped (3 cups) (1 1/4 lbs.)
12 corn tortillas, torn into pieces
1 medium onion, chopped
8 oz. Cheddar cheese, grated (2 cups)

1. Place first four ingredients in medium bowl. Mix well.
2. Make 2 layers of ingredients in a sprayed 9" x 13"
   pan in this order: chicken, tortilla pieces, onion,
   soup mixture, cheese. Repeat layers.
3. Bake uncovered 45 - 60 minutes at 325° (300° -
   glass pan).

6 - 8 servings.

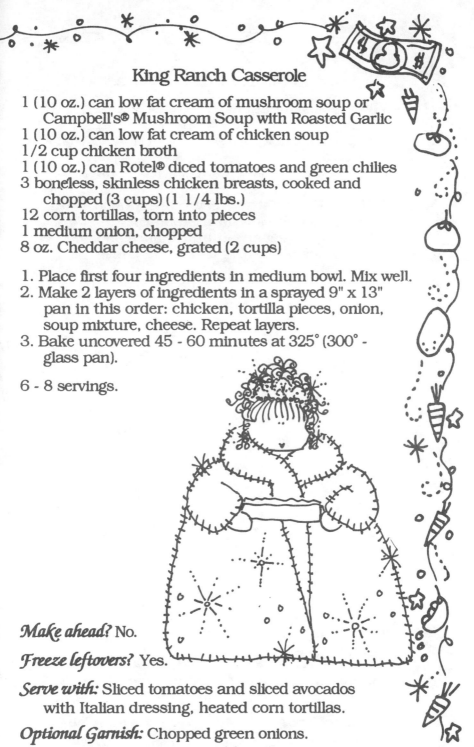

Make ahead? No.

Freeze leftovers? Yes.

Serve with: Sliced tomatoes and sliced avocados
    with Italian dressing, heated corn tortillas.

Optional Garnish: Chopped green onions.

Company Chicken Casserole

3 boneless, skinless chicken breasts, cooked and
  chopped (3 cups) (1 1/4 lbs.)
1 (6 oz.) box Uncle Ben's® Long Grain and Wild Rice,
  cooked
1 (10 oz.) can low fat cream of celery soup
1 medium onion, chopped
2 (15 oz.) French style green beans, drained
1 cup Hellman's® low fat mayonnaise
1 (8 oz.) can water chestnuts, drained and chopped
6 oz. Cheddar cheese, grated (1 1/2 cups)

1. Place all ingredients in large bowl and mix well.
2. Place mixture in sprayed 9" x 13" baking dish.
3. Bake uncovered 25 - 30 minutes at 350°
   (325° - glass pan).

8 servings.

Make ahead? Only a few hours ahead. Refrigerate.

Freeze leftovers? No.

Serve with: Canned fancy chunky mixed fruit, drained
and mixed with vanilla yogurt or a gelatin salad.
Oversize biscuits from dairy case.

Optional Garnish: Chopped slivered almonds or
pimientos.

14

Johnny Mazetti

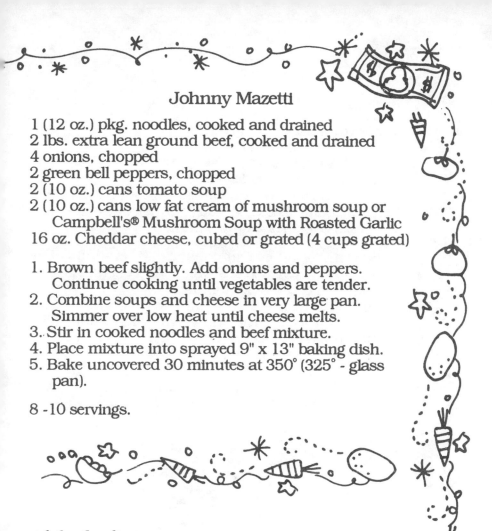

1 (12 oz.) pkg. noodles, cooked and drained
2 lbs. extra lean ground beef, cooked and drained
4 onions, chopped
2 green bell peppers, chopped
2 (10 oz.) cans tomato soup
2 (10 oz.) cans low fat cream of mushroom soup or
    Campbell's® Mushroom Soup with Roasted Garlic
16 oz. Cheddar cheese, cubed or grated (4 cups grated)

1. Brown beef slightly. Add onions and peppers.
   Continue cooking until vegetables are tender.
2. Combine soups and cheese in very large pan.
   Simmer over low heat until cheese melts.
3. Stir in cooked noodles and beef mixture.
4. Place mixture into sprayed 9" x 13" baking dish.
5. Bake uncovered 30 minutes at 350° (325° - glass
   pan).

8 - 10 servings.

Make ahead? Can be partly assembled a day ahead.
Cook noodles and mix with beef mixture at baking time.

Freeze leftovers? Yes.

Serve with: Salad on a stick. Arrange these on individual wooden skewers: fresh broccoli florets, large pitted
black olives, cherry tomatoes, fresh mushrooms. Lay
completed skewers in a loaf pan and cover with Italian
dressing. Chill 20 minutes to 2 hours, turning every
20 minutes. Serve on skewers - each person removes
their salad from skewer. Garlic bread (purchased or
homemade.)

Optional Garnish: Sliced green bell pepper rings.

15

Mexican Casserole

1 lb. extra lean ground beef
1 (14 oz.) can diced tomatoes
1 (1 oz.) packet taco seasoning mix
1 (10 oz.) can enchilada sauce
1 (12 oz.) carton fat free cottage cheese (1 1/2 cups)
8 oz. Cheddar cheese, grated (2 cups), divided
1 (10 oz.) bag tortilla chips, broken

1. Brown ground beef in nonstick skillet, drain off fat.
2. Add tomatoes, taco seasoning, and enchilada sauce.
   Simmer, covered, 20 minutes.
3. Mix cottage cheese with half the cheddar.
4. Layer in this order in sprayed 9" x 13" baking dish:
   half the tortilla chips, half the meat mixture
   all the cheese mixture
   remaining tortilla chips, remaining meat mixture
   top with remaining grated cheddar.
5. Bake uncovered 30 minutes at 350° (325°- glass
   pans).

6 - 8 servings.

Make ahead? Can be partly assembled a day ahead.
Layer ingredients when ready to bake.

Freeze leftovers? Yes.

Serve with: Guacamole served on torn lettuce.
Buy or make guacamole (dairy case or freezer).
Cornbread twists from dairy case.

Optional Garnish: Finely crushed tortilla chips.

16

Chiles Rellenos Casserole

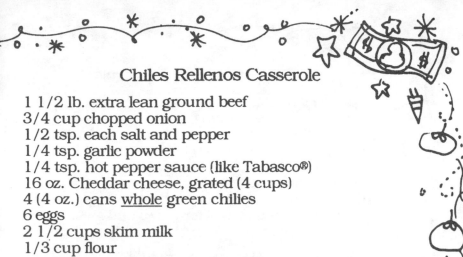

1 1/2 lb. extra lean ground beef
3/4 cup chopped onion
1/2 tsp. each salt and pepper
1/4 tsp. garlic powder
1/4 tsp. hot pepper sauce (like Tabasco®)
16 oz. Cheddar cheese, grated (4 cups)
4 (4 oz.) cans <u>whole</u> green chilies
6 eggs
2 1/2 cups skim milk
1/3 cup flour
picante sauce to serve

1. Brown ground beef and chopped onion in large nonstick skillet. Drain off fat. Add seasonings.
2. Slice open chiles. Remove seeds. Flatten chiles, cut into 1" squares and arrange half of them in sprayed 9" x 13" baking dish.
3. Top with half the cheese and all the meat mixture.
4. Place remaining chiles on top of casserole and top with remaining cheese.
5. Place eggs, milk and flour in large bowl. Beat well with a fork. Pour this evenly over casserole.
6. Bake uncovered 45 to 60 minutes at 350° (325°- glass pan) until mixture is set. Serve with picante sauce.

6 - 8 servings.

Make ahead? Can partly assemble a day ahead. Make the egg mixture and pour over casserole when ready to bake.

Freeze leftovers? Yes.

Serve with: Guacamole (homemade or purchased - dairy case or frozen), canned black beans with jalapenos.

Optional Garnish: Chopped Roma tomatoes.

Beef Enchilada Casserole

1 lb. extra lean ground beef
1 (1 oz.) pkg. taco seasoning
6 corn tortillas, torn into quarters
2 (15 oz.) cans Ranch Style® beans, drained
8 oz. Cheddar cheese, grated (2 cups)
4 green onions, chopped
1 (10 oz.) can low fat cream of chicken soup
1 (10 oz.) can diced Rotel® tomatoes and green
    chilies, drained

1. Brown ground beef, drain off fat, mix in taco
   seasoning.
2. Overlap tortillas over bottom of sprayed 9" x 13"
   casserole pan.
3. Spread beef mixture over tortillas. Top with beans.
4. Sprinkle with most of the cheese. Top with onions.
5. Mix soup and tomatoes and pour over casserole.
   Cover with foil.
6. Bake 50 - 60 minutes at 350° (325° - glass pan).
   Remove casserole from oven, uncover and top
   with remaining cheese.

This can also be made with 3 cups chopped, cooked
chicken meat (3 boneless, skinless chicken breasts -
1 1/4 lbs.), instead of ground beef.

6 - 8 servings.

Make ahead? Can partly assemble a day ahead.
Pour soup and tomato mixture over casserole
when ready to bake.

Freeze leftovers? Yes.

Serve with: Guacamole (homemade or purchased-
dairy case or frozen), topped with sliced Roma
tomatoes and sliced green onions, heated corn
tortillas with butter.

Optional Garnish: Sliced black olives.

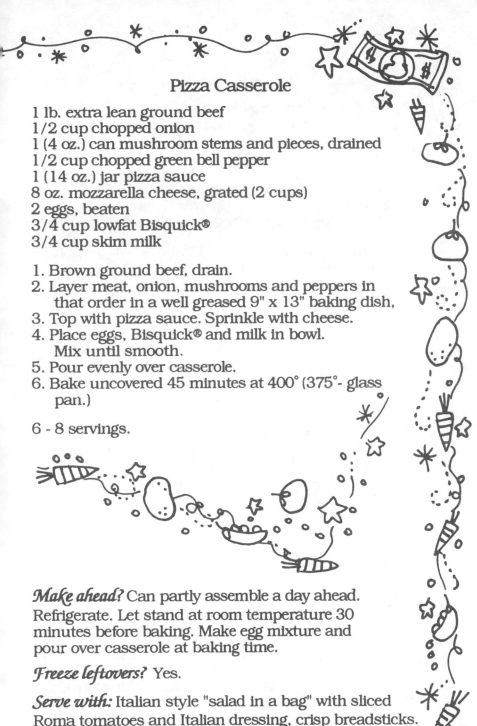

Pizza Casserole

1 lb. extra lean ground beef
1/2 cup chopped onion
1 (4 oz.) can mushroom stems and pieces, drained
1/2 cup chopped green bell pepper
1 (14 oz.) jar pizza sauce
8 oz. mozzarella cheese, grated (2 cups)
2 eggs, beaten
3/4 cup lowfat Bisquick®
3/4 cup skim milk

1. Brown ground beef, drain.
2. Layer meat, onion, mushrooms and peppers in that order in a well greased 9" x 13" baking dish,
3. Top with pizza sauce. Sprinkle with cheese.
4. Place eggs, Bisquick® and milk in bowl. Mix until smooth.
5. Pour evenly over casserole.
6. Bake uncovered 45 minutes at 400° (375°- glass pan.)

6 - 8 servings.

Make ahead? Can partly assemble a day ahead. Refrigerate. Let stand at room temperature 30 minutes before baking. Make egg mixture and pour over casserole at baking time.

Freeze leftovers? Yes.

Serve with: Italian style "salad in a bag" with sliced Roma tomatoes and Italian dressing, crisp breadsticks.

Optional Garnish: Sliced green bell pepper rings.

Almost Instant Lasagne

1 medium onion, chopped
1 1/2 lbs. extra lean ground beef
1 (26 oz.) jar spaghetti sauce
1 Tb. Italian seasoning
1 1/4 cups water
1 (16 oz.) carton cottage cheese (2 cups)
12 oz. mozzarella cheese, grated (3 cups)
1 (8 oz.) pkg. lasagne noodles (9 noodles), uncooked

1. Brown onion and ground beef in very large pan
   for 3 minutes. Drain off fat.
2. Add spaghetti sauce, seasoning and water. Mix well.
3. Mix cottage cheese and mozzarella in medium bowl.
4. Layer ingredients in sprayed 9" x 13" baking dish in
   this order:
   3 uncooked lasagne noodles, meat, cheese
   3 more noodles, meat, cheese
   last 3 noodles, meat, cheese.

   This expands to fill the pan as it cooks.
5. Cover very tightly with foil. Place pan on a baking
   sheet to catch any drips. Bake 1 hour at 350°
   (325° for glass pan). Remove from oven. Let stand
   covered for 30 minutes before serving (important -
   it finishes cooking during this time.)

6 - 8 servings.

Make ahead? Make up to 2 hours before baking.
Don't refrigerate.

Freeze leftovers? Yes.

Serve with: Gazpacho salad - Mix 3 chopped tomatoes,
4 chopped green onions, 1 (4 oz.) can chopped green
chilies, 1 (4 oz.) can chopped black olives, 3 Tb. olive
oil, 1 tsp. garlic powder and 1 Tb. red wine vinegar.
Serve this over a lettuce leaf or torn lettuce. Garlic
bread (homemade or purchased).

Optional Garnish: Fresh parsley.

Reuben Casserole

1 (8 oz.) pkg. wide noodles, cooked
1/2 stick margarine
1 (15 oz.) can sauerkraut, drained
1/2 lb. corned beef from the deli, chopped
2 medium tomatoes, finely chopped
1/2 cup Thousand Island dressing
12 oz. Swiss cheese, grated (3 cups)
6 Ry-Krisp® crackers, processed into crumbs
1/2 tsp. caraway seed (opt.)

1. Add margarine to hot noodles. Spread this in sprayed 9" x 13" baking dish.
2. Top with sauerkraut, corned beef and tomatoes in that order.
3. Dot with Thousand Island dressing, sprinkle evenly with grated cheese.
4. Top with cracker crumbs and caraway seeds.
5. Cover with foil.
6. Bake 40 minutes at 350° (325°- glass pan). Uncover and bake 10 more minutes.

6 - 8 servings.

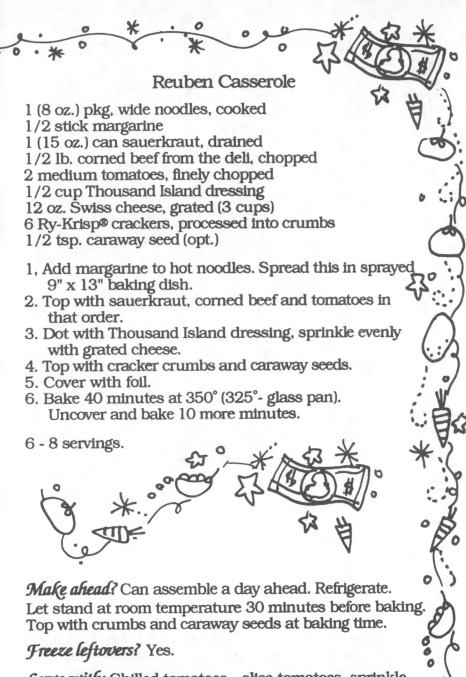

Make ahead? Can assemble a day ahead. Refrigerate. Let stand at room temperature 30 minutes before baking. Top with crumbs and caraway seeds at baking time.

Freeze leftovers? Yes.

Serve with: Chilled tomatoes - slice tomatoes, sprinkle very lightly with sugar, top with Italian dressing. Chill. Party rye bread - heated and buttered.

Optional Garnish: Slice a Roma into 6 or 8 small wedges.

Red Beans and Rice

1 bunch green onions, chopped
3 stalks chopped celery
3/4 cup chopped green bell pepper
1 stick margarine
1 (14 oz.) pkg. Healthy Choice® smoked sausage
    (2 large links). thinly sliced
2 (15 oz.) cans red beans, drained
3 cups cooked rice (1 cup before cooking)
1 (14 oz.) can chicken broth - this is a large can
1/2 tsp. chopped garlic (from a jar - or chop fresh)

1. Sauté onions, celery and bell pepper in margarine
   in very large nonstick pan 10 minutes, stirring often.
2. Add sliced sausage, beans and cooked rice. Mix well.
3. Place mixture in sprayed 9" x 13" baking dish.
4. Pour chicken broth over all.
5. Bake uncovered 25 minutes at 350° (325°- glass
   pan).

6 - 8 servings.

Make ahead? Can be assembled a day ahead.
Pour chicken broth over casserole at serving time.

Freeze leftovers? Yes.

Serve with: Fruit salad on a stick - place fresh
strawberries, seedless grapes, peeled kiwi chunks,
sliced bananas on wooden skewers (break skewers
to 8" long). Lay prepared skewers in a loaf pan.
Pour 1/2 cup poppy seed dressing (purchased) over
them. Chill 30 minutes up to 2 hours. Also serve
with cornbread muffins (homemade or frozen.)

Optional Garnish: Chopped fresh parsley.

Creamy Potato Ham Casserole

1 (32 oz.) bag frozen hash brown potatoes, thawed
1 stick margarine, melted
1/4 cup finely chopped onion
1 (10 oz.) can low fat cream of chicken soup
1 (16 oz.) carton light sour cream (2 cups)
8 oz. Cheddar cheese, grated (2 cups)
1 - 2 lbs. low fat ham, cut into 1/2" cubes
1/3 cup Italian bread crumbs (homemade or from
   a canister)

1. Place all ingredients except bread crumbs in very
   large pan and mix well.
2. Place mixture in 9" x 13" baking pan.
   Top with bread crumbs.
3. Bake uncovered 1 hour at 350° (325°- glass pan).

6 - 8 servings.

This is good for dinner or breakfast. Use 1 lb. ham
for a breakfast casserole and 2 lbs. ham for dinner.

Make ahead? Can be assembled a day ahead.
Refrigerate. Let stand at room temperature
30 minutes before baking.

Freeze leftovers? Yes.

Serve with: Fresh orange segments (good sprinkled with
mint extract) or a fruit salad, broccoli or sugar snap
peas (frozen). Cornbread muffins (homemade or frozen).

Optional Garnish: Canned French fried onions.

Show-Off Seafood Casserole

1 1/2 sticks margarine, divided
1/2 cup finely chopped onion
1/2 cup finely chopped green bell pepper
1 (10 oz.) can low fat cream of mushroom soup
1 (4 oz.) can mushroom stems and pieces, drained
1 cup skim milk
3 cups cooked rice (1 cup before cooking)
1 lb. cooked, peeled shrimp (can buy cooked shrimp
  and cut off the tails or cook your own)
1 (6 oz.) can crab meat, picked over carefully for bits
  of shell
1 cup seasoned bread crumbs (homemade or from a can)
4 oz. sharp Cheddar cheese, grated (1 cup)

1. Melt 1/2 stick margarine in large nonstick pan.
   Sauté onion and bell pepper for 5 minutes,
   stirring constantly
2. Add soup, mushrooms and milk. Cook, covered,
   over low heat for 10 minutes, stirring often.
3. Add cooked rice.
4. Add crab meat and shrimp (cut shrimp in half if large)
5. Place mixture in sprayed 9" x 13" baking dish.
6. Spread crumbs evenly over top of casserole.
   Pour 1 stick melted margarine over crumbs.
7. Top with grated cheese.
8. Bake uncovered 45 minutes at 350° (325°- glass
   pans).

6 - 8 servings.

Make ahead? No.

Freeze leftovers? No.

Serve with: Place pineapple slices on salad plates.
Sprinkle with fresh lime juice and a speck of ginger.
Top with a spoonful of mayo. Also serve sugar snap
peas or broccoli spears (frozen) and crescent rolls.

Optional Garnish: Chopped slivered almonds and fresh
parsley.

24

Shrimp Eleganté

1 green bell pepper, finely chopped
4 stalks celery, finely chopped
1 bunch green onions, finely chopped
1 medium onion, chopped
1 stick margarine
1/2 cup flour
1 (16 oz.) carton half and half (2 cups)
16 oz. hot Velveeta® Mexican cheese, cubed or
    grated (4 cups), (or buy grated Velveeta®)
1 (12 oz.) pkg. curly noodles, cooked
1 (4 oz.) can mushroom stems and pieces, drained
2 lbs. cooked shrimp (cook your own or buy boiled
    shrimp and remove tails)
2 Tb. grated Parmesan

1. Sauté pepper, celery, green onions and onion in
   margarine in large nonstick pan over low heat
   for 10 minutes or until tender.
2. Stir in flour and half and half. Cook over low
   heat, stirring constantly until thickened.
3. Add cubed Velveeta® and stir until melted.
4. Add cooked noodles, mushrooms and shrimp.
   Mix gently.
5. Place mixture into a sprayed 9" x 13" baking
   dish. Sprinkle with Parmesan.
6. Bake uncovered 20 minutes at 350° (325°-
   glass pans).

6 - 8 servings.

Make ahead? No.

Freeze leftovers? No.

Serve with: Blue Cheese Pears - Wash and slice ripe
pears in half. Remove seeds and core. Mix 1/2 cup
cream cheese with 2 Tb. blue cheese crumbles.
Place this mixture in pear cavities. Chill.
Also serve asparagus or broccoli spears.

Optional Garnish: Chopped slivered almonds.

Creamy Crab Casserole

1 (10 oz.) can low fat cream of mushroom soup
1/4 cup sherry
1/4 cup low fat half and half
3 tsp. Worcestershire sauce
8 oz. sharp Cheddar cheese, grated (2 cups), divided
1/4 tsp. pepper
2 (10 oz.) pkgs. frozen chopped spinach, thawed
    and well drained
2 (6 oz.) cans crabmeat, drained and picked over
    carefully to remove cartilage
1/4 cup unseasoned breadcrumbs (from a canister
    or homemade)
1 Tb. margarine, melted
paprika (opt.)

1. Place first 6 ingredients, using only 1 cup grated cheese, in medium pan. Cook over medium heat, stirring constantly until cheese melts.
2. Place thawed, well drained spinach in medium bowl. Add 1/2 cup cheese mixture and mix well.
3. Spread half the spinach in a well sprayed 8" square baking pan. Top with half the crab. Repeat layers.
4. Pour remaining cheese mixture over the casserole.
5. Combine breadcrumbs with melted margarine and sprinkle over top of casserole.
6. Top with remaining cup of grated cheese.
7. Bake uncovered 15 minutes at 350° (325°- glass pan), cover and bake 10 more minutes.

6 servings.

Make ahead? No.

Freeze leftovers? No.

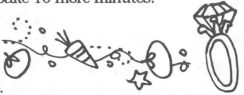

Serve with: Fresh oranges and grapefruit sections (good with a little mint extract sprinkled over or fresh limes squeezed over) or a gelatin salad, dinner rolls.

Optional Garnish: A Roma tomato cut into 6 - 8 small wedges.

Casseroles for Brunch
Sausage Cheddar Casserole

6 slices white sandwich bread, crusts removed and
    bread torn into pieces
1 (4 oz.) can mushroom stems and pieces, drained
1 lb. hot bulk sausage
8 oz. Cheddar cheese, grated (2 cups)
1 (8 oz.) can sliced water chestnuts, drained and
    chopped
1/2 tsp. dry mustard
6 eggs, lightly beaten
1/4 tsp. salt
2 cups skim milk

1. Brown sausage in nonstick pan. Drain off fat
    and crumble sausage.
2. Mix all ingredients in large bowl.
3. Pour into well greased 9" x 13" baking dish.
    Cover with foil and refrigerate overnight.
4. Bake covered 1 hour at 350° (325°- glass pan).

6 - 8 servings.

Make ahead? Must be assembled a day ahead.

Freeze leftovers? Yes.

Serve with: Fresh fruit salad sprinkled with chopped
crystallized ginger (spice section) and honey,
assorted mini muffins (homemade or bakery),
fresh orange juice (buy or squeeze).

Optional Garnish: Arrange some of the mushroom pieces on
top before baking or garnish with fresh parsley.

Casseroles for Brunch
Green Chile Brunch Casserole

6 flour tortillas
1 (4 oz.) can chopped green chiles, drained
1/2 lb. low fat ham, chopped finely
16 oz. Monterey Jack cheese, grated (4 cups)
5 eggs
2 cups skim milk
1 tsp. salt

1. Cover bottom of well sprayed 9" x 13" baking dish with tortillas, cutting to fit.
2. Layer half the chiles, half the ham and half the cheese. Repeat layers.
3. Place eggs, milk and salt in medium bowl. Mix well with a fork. Pour over casserole.
4. Refrigerate at least 1/2 hour or up to overnight.
5. Bake uncovered for 45 to 55 minutes at 350° (325°- glass pan).

6 - 8 servings.

Make ahead? Can be assembled a day ahead. Refrigerate. At baking time, place cold casserole in preheated oven.

Freeze leftovers? No.

Serve with: Fresh fruit with honey, mini cornbread muffins (homemade or bakery), fresh orange juice (buy or squeeze).

Optional Garnish: A Roma tomato cut into 6 - 8 small wedges.

Casseroles for Brunch
Chilequiles

1 large onion, chopped
2 Tb. oil
3 (14 oz.) cans diced tomatoes, undrained
2 (7 oz.) cans chopped green chilies
1/4 tsp. garlic powder (opt)
1/8 tsp. ground cumin (opt.)
1/8 tsp. salt
1 (10 oz.) bag tortilla chips, broken
12 eggs, beaten
1 1/2 lbs. Monterey Jack cheese, grated (6 cups)
2 cups light sour cream
6 green onions, chopped

1. Heat oil in large nonstick pan. Add onions and cook
   3 minutes, stirring constantly.
2. Add tomatoes, chiles and seasonings. Cook over
   low heat until most liquid has evaporated (20
   minutes), stirring often.
3. Place half the tortilla chips in 9" x 13" baking dish.
   Top with half the sauce, half the cheese and all eggs.
4. Top with remaining sauce, then cheese. Spread
   sour cream over top and sprinkle with onions.
5. Bake uncovered 40 - 45 minutes at 350° (325°- glass
   pan) or until eggs are set.

6 - 8 servings. This doesn't freeze well and can't be
              made ahead.

Chicken Chilequiles

   Cook 3 boneless chicken breasts (1 1/4 lbs.) and
chop finely. Make the sauce above in a very large
pan. Add the cooked chicken and simmer in the
sauce as the sauce thickens.
   This won't fit in one 9" x 13" pan. Plan to
make that size pan and a smaller (8" square) pan.
The smaller pan will be done sooner.

Casseroles for Dessert

Bread Pudding

1 large loaf French bread, torn in 1" cubes
1 qt. skim milk (4 cups)
1/2 cup sugar
1 stick margarine, cut in quarters
6 eggs
1 cup raisins
1/2 tsp. cinnamon
1/2 tsp. nutmeg
1 Tb. vanilla

1. Preheat oven to 375°.
2. Place bread cubes in sprayed 9" x 13" baking dish. Place pan in oven for only 2 minutes.
3. Place milk, sugar and margarine in large nonstick pan. Heat over medium heat until margarine is melted and milk is hot, stirring often.
4. Place eggs, raisins, cinnamon and nutmeg in large bowl. Mix with a fork.
5. Add egg mixture to warm milk. Mix well. Add vanilla.
6. Place bread cubes in very large pot. Pour milk mixture over. Stir very lightly from the bottom up.
7. Generously grease (with shortening) a 9" x 13" pan, including sides. Spread mixture evenly in pan.
8. Bake uncovered 30 - 40 minutes at 375° (350° - glass pan). Pour sauce over cooked bread pudding.

Sauce

1 stick margarine
1 cup powdered sugar
1 egg yolk
1/4 cup apple juice or Amaretto liqueur or Bourbon

1. Over low heat, melt margarine with powdered sugar, stirring constantly.
2. Add liquid and egg yolk. Heat over low heat 1 to 2 minutes.
3. Poke holes evenly in hot bread pudding. Pour sauce over. Let stand 10 minutes. 8 - 10 servings.

Casseroles for Dessert
Peach Cobbler

1 stick margarine, melted
1 cup self rising flour
1 cup sugar
1 cup skim milk
2 (29 oz.) cans sliced peaches, drained
    (or 5 cups peeled, sliced fresh peaches tossed
    with 1/2 cup additional sugar)
1/2 tsp. cinnamon

1. Pour melted margarine over the bottom of a
    9" x 13" baking dish.
2. Mix flour, sugar and milk until well blended.
    Pour this mixture evenly over melted margarine.
3. Lay peaches on top of flour mixture.
    Sprinkle with cinnamon.
4. Bake uncovered 1 hour at 350° (325°- glass pan).

6 - 8 servings.

*Select a casserole that bakes for an hour at 350° and put
this right in the oven with it.*

Cinnamon Apple Dump Cake

2 (21 oz.) cans apple pie filling
1 spice cake mix
1 tsp. cinnamon
1 cup chopped pecans
2 sticks margarine, melted

1. Place ingredients in 9" x 13" pan in this order:
    pie filling, half the dry cake mix, cinnamon,
    pecans and remaining dry cake mix.
2. Drizzle evenly with margarine.
3. Bake uncovered 10 minutes at 450°. Lower heat
    to 350° and bake 30 to 35 more minutes.

6 - 8 servings.

Index

Dinner in a Dish

1 lb. stew meat, cut into bite-sized pieces.
1 (10 oz.) can low fat cream of mushroom soup
1 packet dry onion soup mix

1. Place stew meat into 9" square pan.
2. Cover with mushroom soup.
3. Top with dry onion soup mix.
4. Cover tightly with foil.
5. Bake 3 hours at 325° (300°- glass pan).